DIALECT MONOLOGUES

DIALECT MONOLOGUES

Roger Karshner & David Alan Stern

Dramaline Publications®

Dramaline Publications
36-851 Palm View Road
Rancho Mirage, CA 92270
Phone 619/770-6076 Fax 619/770-4507

CONTENTS and TAPE ORDER

FOREWORD

I am delighted to work with Dramaline Publications in recording my performances of Roger Karshner's speeches. Mr. Karshner's monologues, scenes, and plays have been read and performed by tens of thousands of professional and amateur actors. I have often seen his books and my dialect tapes next to each other on the shelves of theater and film bookstores. Now it is a pleasure to see both of our names on the cover of the same product. It has been a delight to perform monologues of this caliber. I sincerely hope my performances do justice to Mr. Karshner's material and increase your interest in dialects and in the art of dialect acting.

DAVID ALAN STERN

SOME THOUGHTS ABOUT DIALECT ACTING

by David Alan Stern

Many of the dialect performances you hear in American films and on television are truly embarrassing. A large number of these performances contain so many linguistic errors that they sound totally fake or "put on." At other times accents may sound real, but they don't correctly correspond to the characters' first languages or regional origins. And often, even when the correct patterns are performed accurately, actors fail to integrate them into fully-developed, believable characters. Creating artistic, authentic-sounding accents is neither a quick nor easy process.

It takes a great deal of time to learn one accent, and even though this book cannot provide you with detailed training in each of the thirteen accents, I do want to lead off with some general information about creating dialect patterns, and, more important, integrating them into complete acting performances. If you are interested in pursuing in depth the art of dialect acting, you may wish to take advantage of some of the twenty-five training programs (cassettes and manuals) available in my *Acting with an Accent* series. You'll find a complete list and ordering information at the back of this publication.

The Technical Part of Acting:

A small percentage of actors can imitate really well; they have the "gift of the parrots" when it comes to accents and dialects. These people can hear almost any speech pattern and reproduce it immediately—usually without having to analyze a single aspect of what they are doing. But, as I said, very few actors have this gift. Others need a more systematic approach. But just being systematic does not guarantee success. Many actors have spent long periods of intensive study without ever approaching an authentic-sounding dialect performance. This kind of failure usually occurs when actors study only the pronunciation changes necessary for the new dialect without addressing some of the other speech traits which add to dialect authenticity.

Pronunciation:

Most texts, recorded instructional programs, and speech specialists concentrate almost exclusively on drilling the vowel and consonant differences between the actor's own speech and the target pattern. Now don't get me wrong—correct pronunciation is important, *but it is not sufficient* for creating the impression of authenticity. Actors who study only the phonetic pronunciation will usually fall far short of the mark. To produce the impression of an authentic accent you must begin by changing two other factors first. I call these elements "muscularity" and "intonation."

Muscularity (Resonance Focus):

The most important part of a dialect's essence comes from its overall resonance or voice focus. Such differences in tone exist because every language of dialect uses a slightly different speech muscularity—a unique style of movement in lips, tongue, and soft palate. Within any given accent or dialect, the characteristic resonance is always noticeable, on all words and phrases, regardless of whether they actually change in pronunciation. In fact, once an actor has mastered the new muscularity and tone focus, many of the important pronunciation changes will happen more easily and be more convincing. Without the proper muscularity and resonance something very organic is missing, so even "correct" pronunciations will often fail to sound correct.

Intonation (Pitch Change):

"Pitch" can refer to any of the several vocal traits. But the pitch changes which take place *inside* vowels are most important for authenticity in many of the accents I teach. In some accents the pitch glides up during the stressed syllables of important words. In others the pitch glides down. In still others the pitch can glide up and then back down within the same stressed vowel. Proper vowel lilt is necessary for authenticity, and for many dialects—such as Irish and American Southern—these pitch glides become tools through which the characters express themselves.

The Artistic Part of Dialect Acting:

Once you have learned the technical skills for producing an authentic-sounding dialect, you must face the realization that technical proficiency is not enough. Too many actors think that "putting on an accent" and "acting with an accent" are the same. They are not! New speech patterns must be integrated into *complete acting performances*.

Dialect actors must avoid going so far within certain speech traits that they end up creating ethnic or linguistic stereotypes. You must make your choices about each individual character on the basis of the script and your own range of experiences. You cannot get caught in a specific personality or emotional state simply because you are using a given speech pattern. Language or dialect background does not dictate character actions. Characters with accents must have the same range of choices available to them as characters whose speech is identical to yours.

Actors must also avoid calling attention to the act of creating a dialect. Remember, the characters aren't putting anything on. They really speak this way; they have no choice. So you must not let the audience observe you thinking about your speech pattern.

You must follow the same principles of "action-reaction" or "moment-to-moment" processing that an artful actor uses in any non-dialect performance. Remember that *acting* is the biggest part of dialect acting. The basic artistic principles do not go away as the speech patterns vary.

So have fun with these monologues. Don't let the accents limit your range of character choices. And don't be limited to my choices either. Whether you are working on these monologues or any other pieces of dramatic material, let the characters' moments become your own.

ABOUT the AUTHORS

David Alan Stern, Ph. D.

After receiving a doctorate in speech from Temple University, David Alan Stern served on the faculties of Wichita State and Penn State Universities and the American Academy of Dramatic Arts. He has been teaching accents to the Hollywood community since 1980. Among his students are: Mike Farrell, Jack Klugman, Edward James Olmos, Bronson Pinchot, and Michael York, as well as Oscar winners Olympia Dukakis and Geena Davis. Dr. Stern's instructional tapes and manuals for learning and reducing accents are used in the speech, theater, and ESL departments of over a thousand colleges and universities and are sold in theater and film book stores throughout the country.

Roger Karshner

Mr. Karshner is a published playwright whose comedies and dramas are produced throughout the United States and Canada. His play *The Dream Crust* was selected by Burns Mantle as one of America's best. He is also the author of eleven drama books which enjoy widespread distribution and sales in the United States, Canada and Great Britain, and are recognized by amateurs and professionals alike as essential for auditions, workshops, and classwork.

SPEECH #1, TEXAS

Here I am speaking with the North-Central Texas dialect of the Dallas region. There is a slight "palatal" resonance caused by a raising of the rear-tongue, along with the characteristic pronunciations of many "American Southern" vowels. There is also a moderate degree of the up and down Southern lilt inside the syllables, though not to the degree that you'd hear it in East and South Texas or in parts of the Southeastern states.

The greatest potential danger with this and other Southern accents is that of "playing the melody" for its own sake instead of having the character use the southern lilt to get important points across to the listeners.

TEXAS

An actor relates audition travails.

So, I go into the studio and read for this here guy who nods and whispers to the other guy who is wearin' director's clothes. You know—like chinos, a blue oxford cloth button-down shirt, two-hundred dollar tennis shoes and one a them stupid little rain hats? Well now the director-type whispers somethin' to this other guy and he whispers somethin' to this skinny woman with hair like a collie dog who looks like she'd gone to one of them eastern schools. Now she looks at me, and she says, "That was really good, could ya do it once more but this time could ya soften your accent a little bit?"

Well . . . hell, I managed t' hold my temper and politely said, "Ma'am, I've just arrived in this town ten days ago, to me it's y'all who have accents. Anyway, this agent sent me in here specifically because you asked for a Texan!" So, I just read it again. Same way I did first time. With them standin' there lookin' real grim like ever'thing in the world right now is hingin' on this little piece of script. But when I finished, she wrote somethin' on a scrap of paper. The other guys looked at what she'd written and nodded. Then they asked me to leave the room an' wait in the hall. Well, an hour later, I had had about enough! I barged in an' asked 'em what the hell was goin' on, an' they said "Lunch." So I set the damned script on fire. Hell, I usta play football against Oklahoma, I know how to deal with animals!

SPEECH #2, IRISH

Irish speech varies as you move to different parts of the island. In fact, the Northern dialect is not even recognized as Irish by most Americans.

My performance contains most of the general Southern Irish vowels. You'll also hear a light frontal resonance (though not the extreme breathiness of some western counties) and the downward-moving vowel lilt (but without the drastic sing-song quality of the Cork region).

As with American Southern patterns, actors always run the risk of "presenting" the Irish lilt rather than using it to get the characters' points across. Be particularly careful not to "make a statement" about the speech pattern you are using. Instead, make statements about what is going on in the life of each particular character.

IRISH

Deep-seated anger as a result of unfeeling parents manifest themselves in a diatribe against a deceased father.

So what? So Da's dyin'! So what's it have to do with me? You go and wallow and blubber if you want to, but not me! I don't want anything to do with the bastards! They're not my family, not the way they treated me! And you, little brother—for Christ's sake, boyo, don't you have any pride at all? They cut

your balls off, those people. They damned near ru-
ined us both. The hell with Da!

Where was he when I was a kid, hmm? Where
was he? Out making deals! Where was he when I
went off the deep end and they dragged me off to the
hospital? Oh, he was in London, or on the continent
somewhere, too busy to come home, too involved
with makin' money, the bastard! And Ma, hell, she
wasn't much better. All she was concerned about
was how my crackin' up would make her look in the
community—in the church. Hell, they didn't raise a
finger, either of 'em. They didn't care.

What's happened to carin'? What's happened to
decency and love and puttin' your flesh and blood
before your goddamned business and clubs and
churches and crap? What ever happened to that,
boyo? Is this what it's all come down to? That
you're born to be a goddamned orphan?

So he dies. So he can die alone, like he let me
live. He's a thoughtless, shallow, rich son of a bitch.
All of 'em are, the whole family. They may have it
in the bank, but they'll never have it where it
counts—in the heart. So you go, you go back if you
want to. Go on back and grovel and wear your best
clothes and fake your sadness and cry and sit around
and get the piss kicked out of your self-esteem. Not
me, not me boyo. I'm not gonna cry for him.

SPEECH #3—STANDARD BRITISH

This is the general, educated dialect heard in the southern part of England. There are many distinctly different speech patterns in the "North Country" and "West Country," and among less educated people of the southern countries.

Standard British speech focuses the sound close to the front of the mouth, uses more pitch glides than American speech, and contains many recognizable pronunciations (especially R-drops and several heavily rounded vowels).

It is very easy to get caught up in an attitude while using this accent. So be careful. Remember that characters are not necessarily "stuffed shirts" just because they're English. British characters can have the same range of attitude as their American cousins. Don't let the sound of the speech pattern determine the choices you will make for your character.

STANDARD BRITISH

Here the actor rails against aging.

Aging! I hate the very thought of it. There are some people in this world who actually think that there are redeeming qualities about aging. About, how do they put it?—"Slipping into one's golden years." Well, forget it! Aging isn't golden, it's brass.

Do you know what aging is actually? I'll tell you. Aging is squinting at the fine print, then finding out that the fine print is a headline. Aging is when your derriere starts drooping below your knees. It's when your most frequent response to any question is— "Would you mind terribly repeating that, old chap?"

Aging is when the latest fashions make you look like a court jester. It's a constant diet of anything that has no flavor whatsoever. It's sitting up straight and holding it in until you get cramps and then finally giving up and buy baggy clothes.

Aging is getting sensible presents for Christmas. And wearing sensible shoes. And keeping sensible hours. It's getting calves as sore as boils from walking more than two blocks. And then, taking the lift instead of walking up one flight. It's remembering never to bend over and touch your toes because you no longer possess a fifth lumbar. It's forgetting to remember not to take calls from people you're trying to forget. It's sticking out your tongue at a "Happiness is Being a Grandparent" bumper sticker and finding out it's on your own car.

Aging is when your remote control switch becomes the most important thing about your telly. It's aches and pains that are way ahead of those extra-strength aspirin compounds, and brown spots on your arms that you can no longer pass off as freckles because they're now the size of old ha'pennies.

And aging is going to your class reunion and finding out you're in the middle of an elephant's burial ground.

Blast! Show me a person who thinks aging is smashing, and I'll show you a liar.

Aging is terrible! It's preposterous! It's a bloody bore!

SPEECH #4, FRENCH

This character accent is that of European French. A French Canadian accent has a totally different muscularity and speech resonance.

Most French characters speaking English as a second language focus the sound near the opening of the throat and nose, thus creating the characteristic French resonance as well as the pronunciations of the French "R" and several vowels.

It is also true that the language and the accent normally stress the final syllables of words. But exercise caution. If you get too obsessed with this stress pattern, you run the risk of calling attention to your mechanics instead of focusing on the character's discoveries and actions.

FRENCH

This speech deals with the deleterious effects of jealousy.

I have told you a million times that I love you. Must I say it again? All right—I love you, I love you, I love you. There—that makes one million and three. Your jealousy is incredible. Will you please, I beg you, relax? Everything is all right, you have nothing to worry about. Just because I stop and talk to people doesn't mean I am looking. After all, I have to live, eh? to speak to others, to interact, to communicate. Just because I live with you does not mean that I'm obligated to cut off all other human contact. Besides, since when have I given you reason to suspect me? I'm home every night, we spend the weekends together—every waking minute, it seems.

Ah! I think that you are suffering intense insecurity due to your parents divorcing when you were a child, and now you are projecting this into our relationship, which is a very unhealthy and destructive business. You must see us as us, as you and me, as two individuals, two separate, special, unique people. Just accept us for us, please. You don't realize how out of control it's become. Like when I danced with those people at the Christmas party. Don't you think you went slightly overboard? I mean, really—spitting into their eggnog. Maybe you should seek professional help to stop your insane jealously before it stops us. Hmm?

SPEECH #5, NEW YORK CITY

There used to be distinct varieties of New York dialects in Brooklyn, the Bronx, and other parts of the metropolitan area. Styles and varieties still exist around the city, but it's not as easy to classify them by borough nowadays.

I'm using what I call a "general New York" pattern. It does not contain a lot of "dese, dems & dose" street pronunciations, but it is still overtly New York. The muscularity pumps the resonance into the low-front mouth, the "R" sounds drop unless they come before vowels, and several are rounded into the lower lip.

Even though the dialect is a bit harsh and muscular, New Yorkers are not necessarily aggressive and/or stupid. Many actors fall into these stereotypes. Don't be one of them.

NEW YORK CITY

A cabbie speaks to a fare, opens interesting psychic vistas.

After awhile ya learn to read faces. Ya learn to spot the people with bucks. Like they've got tips written all over their foreheads. Every now and then, though, ya miss. Like just the other day I picked up this guy wearin' this homburg hat in front of the UN—a diplomat? So I figured a big tip, right? Guess what?

The guy ups and jumps out of the cab at a light and I get stiffed for the fare.

I drive about ten hours a day. That's a long time to sit on your tush. My average speed?—fifteen miles an hour. You don't make time in Manhattan. There are over 900,000 vehicles on this island during the peak business hours. Crazy.

Sometimes the job gets to me, so I pull into Central Park for ten or fifteen minutes and meditate. That surprise ya? Guess you might call me a Zen driver. Well, then after a few minutes I'm ready for the wars again.

It's not a bad job though. Although sometimes, sometimes I think I should have gone to college like my parents wanted. Na, I've still got time to get into somethin' else if I want to. Maybe computers. Yeah, computers. Ya know, we're living in a computer age. People are wearin' down their fingers pushin' buttons. I'm not sure about it though. I don't know, maybe all this technology is gonna dehumanize us. When I go over to my brothers place in the Bronx, ya know his kids are always messin' with that Macintosh Apple of his. They're really glued, you know? You can hardly get 'em away to eat dinner. And they talk real technical, these little kids, soundin' like young Einsteins. Frankly, I don't think it's healthy. When I was their age, I wasn't hangin' around the house thinkin' about microprocessors. I was out on the streets thinkin' about sex like a normal teenager.

Ya know, maybe I'll write someday. I could take some writing classes and boy I could grind out stories about stuff that happens in this cab that would bend your briefcase. It's quite a life. Everybody from hookers to diplomats. Only difference is—the hookers always pay the fare.

SPEECH #6, BOSTON

Slight variations on Boston dialect are heard throughout Eastern New England. This dialect is even replacing the unique "Down East" pattern in many coastal Maine and New Hampshire regions.

Contrary to the beliefs of many Westerners, Boston speech differs strikingly from that of New York, both in resonance and pronunciation. The low-front New York resonance is replaced by the palatal, almost nasal focus in Boston. Many of the rounded and unrounded vowels actually trade places when you move to the opposite ends of the old New Haven Railroad.

Too often actors play Bostonians as "upper class twits" simply because of the erudite dialect sounds. Remember, the dialect cannot dictate a character's personality or emotions.

BOSTON

A writer speaks of childhood and its impact on creativity.

My grandparents' home in Maine was a truly wondrous place. Beautiful. I have fond memories of it. It represented, that great old farm house, it represented a bastion of clarity against the convoluted world. It was a special place, a place like none other. It was our retreat, our citadel, our castle of loving and sharing.

Mom and Dad and I would always drive up there from Boston on all my school holidays. It was a large house. Brick, with walls at least a foot thick and a working fireplace in every room; fireplaces that were seemingly always burning during the colder months, keeping us cozy, insulating from the hostile elements, the capriciousness of the northern New England winters. In that solid old house we felt safe and secure. We felt no harm could ever befall us there. It was like . . . was like a great brick womb.

Yes, I've drawn on that house and those times repeatedly for my novels, using them as background to humanize and color my stories. But this is only one of the many ways that I've been enriched by that experience. Perhaps the most important thing about those days on the farm is that life's inexorable cycle involved you there. Birth and living and death and rebirth and so on. You were part of that. Part of and witness to the cyclical realities. I was lucky, I guess. Lucky to be part of the rich tapestry of those events; events which have helped me immeasurably as a writer. It's in me, part of me always. And I'm glad of it.

SPEECH #7, MOUNTAIN SOUTHERN

This is the "twangy," sometimes nasal variety of Southern speech heard in the Appalachian regions of the Southeast and the mountains of Arkansas and southern Missouri.

In Mountain speech the southern lilt still moves up and down within the stressed syllables. The Mountain dialect also has more elongated vowels than some southern forms. This creates more double and triple vowels than you would hear in the "general" or "plantation" styles of the dialect.

Mountain Southern is very easy to stereotype. Remember that, in and of themselves, the "Hillbilly twang" and drawn-out vowels do not imply anything negative about the intellect of the characters.

MOUNTAIN SOUTHERN

A speech revealing the impact of sequestered, child-hood days.

When I was just a little kid, my mother and I used to take long walks up in them hills; used to go out and walk nearly all day long. Just the two of us, all alone, yeah, just the two of us. Why, we must have moseyed all over them hills, one time or 'nother, covered every inch of 'em. I don't think there's a path up there I ain't been on.

Mama used to take long strides and it was real hard for me to keep up with her sometimes when the grass and weeds were high. But when that happened, she'd always stop and wait for me and take my hand. And when we'd come to fences, she used to pick me up real gentle like and lift me on over to the other side.

She always talked to me as we walked, too. Talked to me like I was a real growed up person, not just some little hillbilly kid. And she'd tell me stories about the hills, about the Indian mounds and the Indians that she'd make sound real mysterious. And her stories would make me scared. But not real bad scared, mind you—good scared like a kid likes to be scared when a parent's nearby and you can reach out and touch 'em.

And sometimes when we walked, she'd put her arm around me and pull me close and wool my head. And then she'd look down at me and pat me on the shoulder and say, "You're a good kid, hon, yep you're a good kid." Yeah, that's what she'd say all right.

SPEECH #8, CHICAGO

Chicago, Detroit, Buffalo, and other many areas around the Great Lakes have very similar speech patterns.

You can hear from my performance that the resonance is slightly palatal and drawn back into my mouth by a retracted tongue position. The "Short-A" vowel (as in "man" "back" and "that") is also drawn out into its harsh, North-Central pronunciation.

The Chicago dialect can often sound harsh, but remember that the Blues Brothers also had their soft-hearted sides.

CHICAGO

Realization of the deep love which had existed between parents.

We drove out to the grave last Sunday for the first time since the funeral, Dad and I. We didn't talk much. We just rode along in silence. What can you say at a time like that?

It was rainin' a fine soft rain, and the cemetery was quiet and green like I'd never seen it before. In fact, I hadn't seen anything like I saw it that day; or felt things like I felt them then either. It was like being born. It was like . . . I don't know.

We parked the car and got out and Dad walked on ahead of me to the grave. He walked carefully out of respect for those buried there, like he didn't want to disrupt anything or intrude. He approached Ma's grave easily, and when he got there he just stood over it, lookin' down at it for a very long time.

When I came along side him, he didn't notice. He was still intent on that fresh grave. He took the carnations that he'd brought along—Ma's favorite— and laid them carefully on the soft, rounded earth; very carefully like you lay something down late at night because you don't want to wake anybody. Then he knelt down, still lookin' at the grave. It was as though he was lookin' right down into the soul of Ma. And then, right then and there, for the first time, I realized what they'd had between 'em—a deep love that connected them and still did, even though she'd gone away.

I'd always known they cared, but I never felt it like this when she was alive. But now, in death, all of a sudden, I could feel it, what they'd had between them, and it was beautiful. All of a sudden, for the first time, I was part of their world.

SPEECH #9, GERMAN

Most natives of Germany who speak English as a second language use very little pitch variety compared to those people whose German language originated in Austria or Switzerland.

German is not guttural or throaty, as many Americans believe. Only the "H" and "R" sounds are produced close to the throat. Its general muscularity and resonance are actually in the low-front part of the mouth, focused against a slightly tensed lower lip.

For obvious historical reasons, we have often seen actors portraying militaristic German stereotypes. This is aided and abetted by the tight muscularity and monotone of the German accent. But don't let the accent sounds make your character choices for you. The full range of personality and emotional choices await you.

GERMAN

Revealed are the deep-seated feelings for a recently departed pet.

I suppose I'm just not as sophisticated as I thought I was. Here I am, a psychologist with training from the best universities of Europe, and I am shattered because of my cat—a mangy old tomcat that I picked up at an animal shelter. Crazy, ya?

But he was company, a friend. He was quietly understanding, he never complained when I rambled on about my problems. He was a noble creature. Cats are, you know. They are most noble and resilient and independent, and loving without being servile.

My neighbors came over and told me last night. They had found Midnight in the hedge near the house. He had obviously been hit by a car. He was still alive, barely. I'm glad I was not there. I don't think I could have stood it. After he died, they arranged for him to be picked up.

I never realized how much emotion there was running between me and that animal.

I have never been an outgoing person, not really. I usually tend to shy away from people,from social situations. Maybe because I deal with troubled people all day. I don't know. I think it's just me; I've always been a loner.

Midnight filled a great void. He was like another person in the house, something living I could talk to. It was as if that cat actually listened, understood. I confided more personal information to Midnight than I have to any other living thing. And I'm going to miss him; his low purring, his hopping into the bed at night, the warmth of his little body next to mine.

I dearly loved that mangy old tomcat.

SPEECH #10, YIDDISH

Yiddish was the language spoken in the isolated Jewish ghettoes of Eastern Europe. Thus, most Jewish immigrants to America spoke English with heavy Yiddish accents. The language is considered a dialect of German, but its alphabet and a good many words originated in Hebrew.

Yiddish requires very relaxed front-mouth muscles, resulting in the absence of almost all "long vowels." It also has a heavy recognizable up and down lilt within the vowels of stressed syllables.

But be careful not to overdo the Yiddish lilt. It should be used to emphasize ideas. Otherwise it becomes a stereotyped "vocal shrug of the shoulders" and seriously limits your ability to create a fully believable character.

YIDDISH

An obsession with work can lead to alienation.

Dammit t' hell, anyway! You're just not getting the point! It's not that I don't have respect for your work. It's just you've become one big obsessed person with your job and computers and fancy high-tech, that's all.

You know, talking to you anymore is like making a visit to Cal Tech? You never let up. It's data this it's printout that, and over people's heads with all the technical. Look, I take an interest in my work too. I like the retail clothing business. But I'm not sitting around all night putting people to sleep with how we mark down socks. And in my business we use regular terms. For a coat we say "Coat," for pants we say "Pants," for Jockey Shorts we say "Jockey Shorts." At least people can focus on what we're talking about without taking a course in big brains from MIT. So give me a break already. Like tonight with the company at dinner. You did a hour and a half on bytes and kilobytes and megabytes to the point where nobody could take a bite. And face it, how many people are interested in how a central processing unit—whatever in heaven's sake that is to begin with—is wired? Who cares? Look, to be perfectly honest and sincere, you're becoming a high-tech pain in the ass. I don't mean to upset you here, but somebody has to say something. You've got to knock it off with this technical and buzzwords and the big deal about your job. Because if you don't, pretty soon the only audience you're going to have is going to consist of *you.* Trust me.

SPEECH #11, SPANISH

Spanish accents can differ drastically in pitch or intonation characteristics, depending on the country or region of origin. Cuban and Puerto Rican accents, for example, are almost monotone, while most Mexican accents have a very identifiable up and down pitch glide.

I've performed this monologue with what I call a "General South American Spanish" accent. It contains some intonation, but few if any pitch glides. The tongue and lips push forward to focus the resonance behind the top teeth in front of the mouth. You will hear few, if any, "short vowels."

Be careful not to be excessive when elongating vowels in this accent. Too may actors concentrate so heavily on some, and make untoward substitutions for others ("Long-E" for "Short-I," for example) that they lose sight of what the characters are actually saying and doing.

SPANISH

Contrition is expressed regarding parental confinement.

I went over again yesterday. I didn't have any idea what it was like, not really. It seemed like such a cheerful place when I checked it out. But . . . but with Mama in there, it is not cheerful at all. But what could I do, you know? I couldn't keep her here any longer. Not like she was. Not in her condition. I couldn't be with her every minute and the expense of a full-time nurse was out of the question.

(Takes up a photograph and examines it with an expression of deep melancholy.) Ah, Mama. Mamacita. You were so beautiful, so loving, so giving. She was the last person you'd think would get this Alzheimer's disease. I guess there is just no way of knowing. Oh, I'm glad Papa was not here to see it—it would break his heart.

The home is the best in the country, too. But it is still a home, it's depressing. Every time I go over there. . . . Well, at least they will be able to keep an eye on her, hmm? And she wandered off twice, you know? The last time in her nightgown. And it was raining. I found her over in the park, staring at the children's swings. Oh God, it was sad. She was always so proud of her appearance.

So I just couldn't take the chances anymore of her wandering off again. God knows what could happen, you know? So I put her in the home. What else could I do? What the hell else could I do?

SPEECH #12, COCKNEY

To be a "real" cockney, someone would have had to grow up in the section of London that is "within the sound of Bow's Bells." But the Cockney pattern is very closely related to almost all London street dialects. Whereas Standard British uses forward muscularity and resonance, Cockney draws the resonance to the back of the mouth with a lot of rear-tongue action. The dialect retains the British R-drop, and, or course, many Cockneys drop initial H's. Cockneys also tend to link consonants from the end of one word to the beginning of the next.

Many Cockneys are extremely difficult to understand. Actors must not take this accent so far that they lose intelligibility. You can maintain a total impression of authenticity and still be understood perfectly.

COCKNEY

A trouper speaks of an antiquated occupation.

I don't have much of an act. Just a few stale songs and a little dancing thrown in so they won't be able to hit a moving target. Nothing worse, my friend, than a stale cabbage in the ole face, let me tell you.

My mum and dad were entertainers and their parents before them. They worked the provinces back in the days when it meant something; when the theaters and music halls were little jewels strung around the neck of Great Britain. Beautiful houses that did two a day and three on Saturday and people flocked in from all over to see the best of the circuits. Like my dad, who was the finest juggler in the country and traveled with my mother as his assistant. They were first-class people with a first-class act.

Now . . . well now it's different. I pick up what ever I can around Birmingham in the pubs and cabarets. But the days of the live entertainer are over, and for the most part I work only occasionally where they haven't got a discotheque. And I pick up the odd quid at weddings here and there or a private party where they like to have a song and dance man because we are such an oddity—a freak of show business, you might say. But I love it. I love it because it's in my blood and I look at myself as a kind of crusader keeping a tradition alive; a tradition of entertainment without amplified music or backgrounds or light shows or electronics. I just get up and sing the old songs and do the old dances without frills or fanfare. I like to think of myself as a piece of living English history, keeping alive the memory of a simpler time.

SPEECH #13, ITALIAN

I performed this piece with a Southern Italian accent. The Northern pattern is quite different and often not even recognized by Americans as being Italian.

You will hear the pitch and staccato rhythm characteristics carrying over from the original language. As with Spanish there will be few if any short vowels, and the resonance will focus toward the front of the mouth.

Be careful not to go too far with the "intrusive vowel," that is, the addition of the "UH" sound after words which end in consonants. Some speakers with heavy accents (especially Sicilians) actually do stick in this vowel, but that can often lead you headlong into a stereotype and turn your attention away from your character's specific moments, choices, and actions.

ITALIAN

A gentle moment in an otherwise barren parental relationship.

Papa, Papa. Dear Papa. He never had time for us— ever. Even Mama, not even her. She was nothing more than his valet, his housekeeper. I never saw him offer her affection. He was a strangely removed, enigmatic man.

As a child I remember him as an elegant vagrant, coming and going in his mannered, indifferent way.

He was merely a transient who had neither time or inclination for his family. He never had time, especially for me—the youngest. Only once. . . .

Yes, there was this one solitary moment. I was quite young, I remember, very very young. And it was this summer while the family was on holiday in Capri. I was playing alone near the sea when suddenly I felt a large, warm, hovering presence as if the sun were at my shoulder. I looked up and there was Papa, standing above me, watching me in silence.

Then, unexpectedly, totally uncharacteristically, he reached down and touched my hair and stroked it. Ever so gently he stroked it. I remember the look in his eyes in particular. And I'll never forget it. For once his eyes did not have that glass-like coldness that deflected penetration. For that moment they were warm and receptive. And for that moment—for that one fleeting moment—I felt safe, and secure, and very much loved.

ORDER DIRECT FROM DRAMALINE

Please write, phone, or fax for a free catalog.

Dramaline Publications
36-851 Palm View Road
Rancho Mirage, CA 92270
Phone 619/770-6076
Fax 619/770-4507

INSTRUCTIONAL CASSETTES
by
DAVID ALAN STERN, PH. D.

I. *Acting with an Accent* (Learning dialects & Accents). One-hour tapes with manuals covering the following dialects: Standard British, Cockney, Northern British, Irish, Scottish, Australian, American Southern, New York City, Boston, Upper Class New England, Down East New England, Chicago & Detroit, Midwest Farm Belt, Four Texas Dialects, Spanish, Italian, French, German, Russian, Yiddish, Polish, Norwegian & Swedish, Farsi (Persian), West Indian & Arabic & Black African, Various American Accents for English Actors. $16.95 each.

II. *Speaking without an Accent* (Reducing Regional Dialects). One-hour tapes and manuals for speakers wanting to reduce any of the following American Regionalisms: New York City (also N. Jersey & Long Island), American Southern (including Mountain Southern & Texas), Pennsylvania and S. Jersey (also Delmarva— DE, DC, MD), Boston (and all of Eastern New England), Chicago-Detroit-Buffalo (and Great Lakes Regions), American Black Dialects (urban & rural), Midwest Farm Belt dialects (non-Southern varieties), and a special tape of learning Elevated American diction. $16.95 each.

III. *The Sound and Style of American English* (Reducing Foreign Accents). Ninety-minute cassettes with manuals for speakers of English as a Second Language wishing to reduce their foreign accents. $29.95 + $5.00 S&H.

IV. *The Speaker's Voice* (A course in aesthtic voice improvement). For those wishing to obtain richer, more pleasant resonance, and create a more powerful voice without strain or tension in the throat. $29.95 + $5.00 S&H.

DIALECT ACCENT ORDERING INFORMATION

BY MAIL: Please specify the name of each tape. Shipping and handling charges: $4.00 1st tape, .50 each additional tape to a maximum of $7.00. Vermont residents add 5% sales tax. Send check or money orer to:

DIALECT ACCENT SPECIALISTS, INC.
PO BOX 44
Lyndonville, VT 05851

To order by phone using your VISA or MASTER CARD please call 800/753-1016.

EMAIL: dasinc@plainfield.bypass.com
http://plainfield.bypass.com/~dasinc/